U S BLUES

Greg Owens

BROADWAY PLAY PUBLISHING INC
224 E 62nd St, NY NY 10065-8201
212 772-8334 fax: 212 772-8358
BroadwayPlayPub.com

U S BLUES

First printing July 2011
I S B N: 978-0-88145-475-8

Book design: Marie Donovan
Page make-up: Adobe Indesign
Typeface: Palatino
Printed and bound in the U S A

CONTENTS

ABOUT THE AUTHOR

Greg Owens was born and raised in rural southern Indiana. He wrote his first play in 1988 as a junior at Indiana State University in Terre Haute. In 1993, he completed the M F A Playwriting at Indiana University in Bloomington, where he studied with Dennis J Reardon. Many of Greg's early works premiered at the Bloomington Playwrights Project, where he also produced and directed several new plays. In the mid-to-late 90s, Greg's plays appeared in various Off-Loop venues in Chicago and were staged by the Subterranean Theater Company in Los Angeles, which produced the world premiere of his full-length play THE LIFE AND TIMES OF TULSA LOVECHILD (TLC) in 1998.

In 2001, the Collaboraction Theater Company production of T L C, directed by Kimberly Senior, earned seven Jefferson award nominations and was named the "Best Off-Loop Play of the Year" by the *Chicago Tribune*. The play has since enjoyed successful productions in more than a half-dozen states, and was published by Broadway Play Publishing Inc in 2004. In 2005, Stage Left Theater in Chicago presented a workshop production of HOME FRONT, Greg's dark comedy about the Iraq war, published by Broadway Play Publishing Inc in 2006.

Greg has also written short political plays and monologues that have been produced by the Subverse

Theatre Company in London, and has written and directed for the touring Vigilante Theater Company, which has performed his work in rural communities throughout Montana, Idaho, Wyoming, and North Dakota.

Greg lives in Bozeman, Montana with his wife Lila Michael and daughters Lorelei and Eiseley. He teaches at Montana State University and mentors local teens through his work with the non-profit Bozeman Youth Initiative. He dedicates this collection of plays to all the audiences, crew members, producers, directors, designers, and actors at all the small theatres that brought them to life.

PASTIME

PASTIME was a Finalist in the 1991 Actors Theater of Louisville National Ten-Minute Play Contest. It was first produced by the Bloomington (Indiana) Playwrights Project in 1992:

JACKSON .... Jason Farmer
JILLIAN .... Amanda Carrithers
CASEY ....Mike Sherman
EDWARD .... Terry L Hornsby
EDITH ....Katherine Ford

Director ....Karen McCann

(The stage is divided into three areas:
JACKSON *and* JILLIAN, EDWARD *and* EDITH, CASEY
CASEY *wears a baseball uniform and holds a baseball bat.)*

JACKSON: I dug up some bones today.

JILLIAN: Excuse me?

JACKSON: In the yard.

JILLIAN: Bones?

JACKSON: I found some bones in the yard.

JILLIAN: Our yard?

JACKSON: Yes.

JILLIAN: How did they get there?

JACKSON: A skull actually.

JILLIAN: A skull.

JACKSON: Human.

JILLIAN: No.

JACKSON: Yes.

JILLIAN: What was a human skull doing in our yard?

JACKSON: I found another one. Later.

JILLIAN: In the yard?

JACKSON: Under the couch.

JILLIAN: Come on.

JACKSON: It's true.

JILLIAN: There are no skulls under our couch.

JACKSON: Not now.

JILLIAN: Stop kidding around.

JACKSON: I put it in the garage.

JILLIAN: You're not funny.

JACKSON: I put all of them in the garage.

JILLIAN: *All* of them?

JACKSON: Yes.

JILLIAN: You found others?

JACKSON: Yes.

JILLIAN: Where?

JACKSON: In the pantry.

JILLIAN: How many?

JACKSON: Seven.

JILLIAN: My God.

(Lights shift to EDWARD *and* EDITH.*)*

EDWARD: Where are my skulls?

EDITH: In the garage.

EDWARD: I looked there.

EDITH: You didn't see them?

EDWARD: They're not there.

EDITH: That's where you keep them.

EDWARD: They're gone.

EDITH: There were nine yesterday.

EDWARD: I know.

EDITH: I don't know what could have happened to them.

EDWARD: You didn't move them?

EDITH: Why would I move them?

EDWARD: I thought you might have.

EDITH: No.

EDWARD: Someone must have stolen them.

EDITH: I don't know who would do that.

EDWARD: They're gone.

EDITH: Oh well.

EDWARD: We've got to find them.

EDITH: They're gone.

EDWARD: They've got to be around here somewhere.

EDITH: There's no reason to get excited.

EDWARD: My skulls are gone!

EDITH: I don't know how they disappeared. You never let them out of your sight for a minute.

EDWARD: My skulls...

EDITH: I'm glad they're gone.

EDWARD: They could have taken anything.

EDITH: Don't worry, dear. We'll get you some new ones.

EDWARD: Those bastards.

(Lights shift to CASEY.)

CASEY: I remember it like it was yesterday. Two men out and nobody on base. It was the bottom of the 9th. And Casey comes up to bat. *(Beat)* I let the first pitch go by. Didn't like the looks of it. "Strike one," the ump says. I dug in. The second pitch was a mile high and way outside. I let it go. "Strike Two." What the hell kinda call is that? Nowhere near the strike zone. "You're blind as a bat," I said. "Strike Two," he says.

(Lights shift to JACKSON and JILLIAN.)

JILLIAN: We've got to get rid of those things.

JACKSON: What things?

JILLIAN: Those skulls.

JACKSON: You don't like them?

JILLIAN: They're making me crazy.

JACKSON: They're just skulls.

JILLIAN: They keep talking to me.

JACKSON: Don't be silly.

JILLIAN: They're talking to me!

JACKSON: What do they say?

JILLIAN: Crazy things. Things I don't understand.

JACKSON: Like what?

JILLIAN: "Hey batter, batter. Batter, batter, swing! Easy out! Hey batter, batter. Batter, batter, swing!"

JACKSON: You need to relax.

JILLIAN: I want them out of here.

JACKSON: Come on. Let's watch the game.

JILLIAN: Hey batter, batter, batter, batter, swing!

(Lights shift to EDWARD *and* EDITH.)

EDITH: *(To audience)* When I was a little girl, my father took me to see a championship boxing match. My mother protested: "That's no place for a little girl," she said. But I went. We sat up close to the ring. The sweat kept flying off their bodies and landing on my face. I could hear the sound of fists slamming up against faces. Fists pounding. Leather slapping. Grunting. Pounding. Slapping. Grunting. Pounding! Pounding! FLESH RIPPING! BONES BREAKING! *(Beat)* "Now that's entertainment," my dad says.

EDWARD: What did you do with those skulls?

EDITH: What dear?

EDWARD: What did you do with them?

EDITH: Nothing.

EDWARD: Don't lie!

EDITH: I haven't seen them.

EDWARD: I want them now!

EDITH: I don't have them.

EDWARD: GIVE ME THOSE SKULLS!

(EDWARD and EDITH square off like two boxers and freeze in this position. Lights shift to CASEY.)

CASEY: He's standing there on the mound. Grinning at me. Making fun of me with his eyes. I shoot him a grin right back: "You don't scare me you little shit." He goes into his wind-up and hurls one right at me. Catches me square in the chin. I rush out to the mound, swingin' my bat at him. He puts his hands up, tryin' to protect himself. And I let him have it. WHAM! Right on the head. (He pantomimes smashing the players' heads with his bat as he names them.) The catcher runs up. WHAM! The infield rushes the mound. And I let 'em have it. WHAM! Second baseman. WHAM! Third base. WHAM! Shortstop. WHAM! First baseman. The outfield! WHAM! WHAM! WHAM! (Beat) I dropped 'em all. (Pause) I look down and my old Louisville Slugger's covered with blood. It's running down onto my hands. I look down at the field and it's soaked with blood and brains. All kinds of brain junk leaking out of their skulls. I'm standin' in it, ankle deep. (Beat) And the fans are goin' nuts. They're laughin' and clappin' and cheerin'. "Hooray! Hooray!" I look down at all of 'em. I spit a wad of chew right in the pitcher's eye. Nobody brushes back the Mighty Casey.

(Lights shift to JACKSON and JILLIAN.)

JACKSON: *(Watching T V)* Get him! Get that son-of-a-bitch! Tackle him! KILL THAT SON-OF-A-BITCH!

JILLIAN: HEY BATTER, BATTER, BATTER, BATTER, SWING! SWING! SWING!

JACKSON: *(Angrily)* PIPE DOWN, WILL YA! I'M TRYING TO WATCH THE GAME! *(Back to T V)* GODDAMN! DID YOU SEE THAT? HE ALMOST TORE HIS HEAD OFF! OH MAN! *(Beat)* I love this game.

(Blackout)

END OF PLAY

FISH BABY DREAMING

FISH BABY DREAMING was first produced by
Abiogenesis Productions at Café Voltaire, Chicago in
1995:

TERESA .... Lila Ann Michael

Director ....Greg Owens

TERESA: I had the dream again. I was sitting in the same waiting room. Suns and stars. Rainbows and unicorns decorating the walls in Crayola 64-box colors. All the magazines are *Humpty Dumpty, Ranger Rick. Jack and Jill.* A crumpled-around-the-edges poster with a warning from Big Bird to look left, then right, then left again hangs on the door to the main office.

A multi-cultural children's choir sings the alphabet song in rounds over the lobby P A. Each round in a new language.

The receptionist hums along and smiles a Mother Goose smile. I know she's the receptionist because it's spelled out in pink and blue building blocks across the front of her desk.

It's all very cute.

And I'm so nervous, I can barely concentrate on the Barney seek-and-find word puzzle I've picked up to distract myself. Suddenly, without warning, the receptionist looks up at me and says:

"The baby will see you now."

"What? Oh. Me. Okay."

She opens the door for me and I walk into the office. That's when I see him for the first time. He's about twenty-three inches tall. Blue eyes. Pinkish complexion. And light blonde hair that I notice is beginning to thicken with advancing age. He smiles at me from behind his desk.

"Please come in," he says. "Have a seat." And so I do. He sits up in his chair and leans toward me. He spreads his palms out in front of him. His chubby little

wrinkly fingers tap the desktop. Finally, he looks right
at me and says:

"So, you desire propagation?"

I nod, weakly. It takes what seems hours to form the
sound at the back of my throat, but I finally manage to
say: "Y-y-y-yes."

At that, he smiles. A...curious smile? Amused? Sinister?
He pushes a red button on the desk and a large black
curtain behind him opens to reveal an enormous fish
tank. Full of water with colored rocks and gurgling
bubbles and phony plastic coral reefs lining the
bottom.

But inside the tank there are no fish. There are babies.
Dozens of soft, pink, little babies. Swimming around.
Bobbing up and down. Diving to the bottom. Staring
through the glass. At me.

I feel something touch my hand. I look down to see
that from across the desk I'm being handed a pink
plunger with a blue handle.

"Go ahead," he says, "try your luck."

I walk toward the tank. Still confused and uncertain.
He stays behind the desk, instructing me through
pantomime until I comprehend the proper procedure.
I climb the small step ladder beside the tank and thrust
the plunger into the water, attaching it to one of their
shiny foreheads.

I haul it out of the water and hold the plunger at
my shoulder as its tiny arms and legs flail in the air,
dripping water onto the carpet floor.

He smiles from behind the desk: "Nice catch," he says.
And I nod.

There is a sudden squoosh of failing suction as the
head of the plunger lets go and the slimy, slippery
nipper falls to the floor. I reach down and try to pick it
up. But it slips and slides out of my hands.

From behind the desk I hear: "Use the tongs."

Again, I find another tool shoved into my hands. A set of stainless steel salad tongs which I use to pick the wriggling creature up off the floor.

As I retrieve it, I see that it is turning blue. Gasping wildly for air. Desperately, I look toward my advisor behind the desk, imploring him to help me.

He looks at me with scorn and snorts: "Breathing *is* important."

With that, the suffocating thing in my hands attaches its mouth to mine and begins to suck the oxygen out of my body. I feel my lungs contract as it steals my air.

From the desk: "Congratulations, Mommy."

Then everything goes black. In the darkness, I feel the babyfish inhaling the last of my breath.

I wake up. Gasping. The baby kicks.

END OF PLAY

EXTREME CUSTOMER SERVICE

EXTREME CUSTOMER SERVICE was first produced by the Bloomington Playwrights Project in 2008. For this production the gender and name of the telemarketer were changed:

SAM ....Josie Gingrich
JANIS .... Andi Haynes
Director .... Pat Anderson.

(Scene: JANIS *sits in a chair reading a magazine.* CHAD *sits in another chair in a different area; he wears a headset telephone piece. He dials a number.)*

(Sound: We hear a phone ring onstage. JANIS *picks up a phone from her lap.)*

JANIS: Hello?

CHAD: *(Reading screen)* Hello, is this Janis?

JANIS: Yes. Who's this?

CHAD: Hi Janis. This is Chad from Computer Cult. How are you today?

JANIS: Is this a sales solicitation?

CHAD: No way, Janis.

JANIS: Why are you calling?

CHAD: I was just calling today to see if there was anything the Computer Cult Technical Support Team could do to help you get more enjoyment and/or productivity from your Computer Cult computer.

JANIS: Wait. You work in Technical Support and you're calling me?

CHAD: That's right.

JANIS: But aren't customers supposed to call you in Technical Support when they have a problem?

CHAD: Well, Janis, that's how some—inferior— companies do it. But here at Computer Cult, we eschew such passive techniques of "traditional" customer service. In our effort to be your full-service technological guidance provider, Computer Cult is willing to do whatever it takes to satisfy your most critical needs—even if that means helping you imagine those needs before they even arise.

JANIS: Wow. That's ambitious.

CHAD: There's no traffic jam on the extra mile, Janis.

JANIS: There's just one thing…

CHAD: How can Computer Cult make it better?

JANIS: Well, I don't know how to answer that exactly because, you see, here's my problem…

CHAD: Problems are wires that just need to be plugged into the right thingy, Janis. Let me help.

JANIS: Chad?

CHAD: Yes, Janis?

JANIS: What I'm trying to tell you is I don't even own a Computer Cult computer.

(Pause)

CHAD: Oh.

JANIS: Yeah.

(Pause)

CHAD: So what are you up to?

JANIS: Excuse me?

CHAD: What does a nice-sounding woman like yourself in *(Reads screen)* Albuquerque, New Mexico do on a Saturday afternoon? You just chillin' or what?

JANIS: Wait. Shouldn't the fact that I just told you I don't own any products from your company necessitate at least an apology, if not an abrupt hang-up?

CHAD: Some other companies would hang up on you just because you didn't buy any of their stuff. But at

Computer Cult, we try to get to know you to figure out why you haven't bought our stuff, and try to persuade you as a friend that there's a lot to be gained for you from owning our stuff. And please don't ask me to apologize for trying to provide you with an extreme customer service experience, Janis. That's just who I am.

JANIS: I really don't want to be rude and slam this phone in your ear.

CHAD: It's okay, Janis. Whatever you have to do is cool with me. I'll go ahead and say "have a nice day" now just in case you do hang up on me.

JANIS: I mean, you're a real person, aren't you?

CHAD: Of course I am.

JANIS: And somehow you can just sit there and say these things on the phone to total strangers. Project this persona. Vomit this corporate babble from your script and pretend that I should think it's perfectly natural to be talking to some humanoid tele-bot about a computer I don't have and don't want. People like you just amaze me.

CHAD: Thanks.

JANIS: I mean, what person in his or her right mind thinks this is a good way to get people to buy their stuff? Invading my private time and personal space with unwanted, unwelcome, unsolicited business calls is tantamount to psychological violation. What marketing guru moron thinks they can get me to buy stuff I don't want by attacking me and taking away my dignity?

CHAD: Well, Janis. I think you'd be surprised to learn just how many satisfied Computer Cult customers have a different view of their relationship with Computer Cult and its Technical Support Team. If you'd like to hear some recorded testimonials from real Computer Cult customers who have nothing but great things to say about Computer Cult, just press one now.

JANIS: This is insane. Do you actually like doing this? Don't you ever feel at least weird about it? Surely this job of yours must damage you in some fundamental ways as a human being. I mean, it can't be good for your soul, right?

CHAD: Actually, Janis, can I tell you something?

JANIS: Is it something that doesn't come from a sales script?

CHAD: It comes directly from the center of my heart.

JANIS: Okay. Tell me.

CHAD: Sometimes I think that my life would have no meaning at all... if it weren't for the joy my heart receives... from helping people like you find the Computer Cult solution that's right for them.

JANIS: I am going to hang up now.

CHAD: You asked for the truth and I told you.

JANIS: So you're honestly telling me that your life has meaning because you talk like a creepy dork about computers all day to total strangers?

CHAD: Yes.

JANIS: Don't people say horrible things and curse at you a lot?

CHAD: Every day.

JANIS: I don't think my self-esteem could withstand that.

CHAD: Don't kid yourself, Janis. You're stronger than you think.

JANIS: Well, I don't know about that.

CHAD: You were strong enough to stand up to me about my creepy dork persona and corporate marketing bullshit.

JANIS: Well, sometimes it's easier to say what's on your mind, or speak up about what you feel, when you're talking to someone you don't know, and you don't care how shitty you make them feel, you know?

CHAD: I do know. That's why I'm here. Anything else you'd like to get off your chest?

JANIS: No, I think I'm good.

CHAD: I know you are.

JANIS: Thanks, Chad.

CHAD: No problem. Hey, listen I'll let you get going. It was great talking with you.

JANIS: You're not going to try to sell me anything else?

CHAD: You said you didn't want anything.

JANIS: Yes, but it isn't your job to make me want things I don't want and then take my credit card number?

CHAD: That would be my job at some—lame— companies. But, at Computer Cult, I'm just Chad and I wanted to say hello, and let you know that if you ever do need anything from us, I won't rest until I make it happen for you.

JANIS: Thanks.

CHAD: You're welcome.

JANIS: That's sweet.

CHAD: You're worth it.

JANIS: Will you call again?

CHAD: Will you?

JANIS: Why not?

CHAD: That's what I'm sayin'.

JANIS: Goodbye.

CHAD: Bye now.

(JANIS hangs up phone. Lights out on JANIS, or actor assumes neutral/out of character position. CHAD dials another number.)

CHAD: *(With southern accent now)* Hey y'all, is this Elmer? Well how-do Elmer? This is Johnny Earl from Computer Cult. How are things down in Loosy-anna today?

(Blackout)

END OF PLAY

THE LEPER VALLEY CONDO ASSOCIATION

THE LEPER VALLEY CONDO ASSOCIATION is unproduced.

(Scene: An office in a condo association. BRYAN *sits at the desk, cheerfully working. Two hooded figures enter.* BRYAN *doesn't notice them at first. The hooded figures look at one another, then one of them knocks on the door.)*

BRYAN: *(Looking up)* Oh. Hi. You must be my two o'clock. Come on in. Have a seat.

(The hooded figures take a seat in front of BRYAN's *desk.* BRYAN *turns away from them for a moment to collect some papers.)*

BRYAN: *(With his back turned)* So, you're here about the opening in 10-D, right? *(Turning around)* Okay— *(Reading their names off paper)* Mister and Mrs Phillips, it's okay. You can take the hoods off in here.

(The hooded figures turn toward one another uncertainly, then slowly pull back the hoods to reveal themselves as CHUCK *and* SHEILA PHILLIPS. *Underneath they look like any normal Yuppie couple, except for the fact that their bodies are covered by large white scaly scabs and festering sores.)*

BRYAN: Hi. I'm Bryan.

*(*BRYAN *waves at* CHUCK *and* SHEILA *instead of offering his hand to shake.)*

CHUCK: Hello Bryan. I'm Chuck Phillips and this is my wife, Sheila.

BRYAN: *(Cordially)* Sheila.

SHEILA: *(Quietly)* Hello.

BRYAN: Welcome to the Leper Valley Condo
Association, the premiere private leper community in
the Northeast.

CHUCK: Thank you.

(SHEILA *nods*.)

BRYAN: Now, before we get started with the application
process, I'd be happy to answer any questions you
might have.

CHUCK: I was wondering if you could tell us a little
more about the surrounding area here. The scenery
was amazing on the drive up.

BRYAN: Yes, it is, isn't it? Well, our grounds cover
approximately two hundred and twenty-five acres
with private access to Lake Hansen and, of course, a
lovely view of the mountains from just about anywhere
on the property.

CHUCK: Excellent.

SHEILA: I—

BRYAN: Yes, Mrs Phillips?

(SHEILA *lowers her head, self-consciously*.)

CHUCK: It's okay, honey.

BRYAN: *(Friendly, compassionate)* Did you have a
question?

SHEILA: *(Quietly)* I was...what about the condos?

BRYAN: Sure. All together, we have a hundred and
eighty-five units at two thousand square feet each.
Washer and dryer included. All new appliances. Wall-
to-wall carpeting. Energy-efficient windows. And a
state-of-the-art electronic security system.

CHUCK: Very nice.

BRYAN: Yes.

SHEILA: Central air?

BRYAN: Of course.

CHUCK: What about cable?

BRYAN: Absolutely.

SHEILA: Housekeeping?

BRYAN: Yes, ma'am.

CHUCK: Jacuzzi?

BRYAN: And sauna.

SHEILA: Parking?

BRYAN: Each unit comes with its own two-car garage.

CHUCK: What about garbage pick up?

BRYAN: Yes, as well as free curbside recycling.

CHUCK: Great.

BRYAN: Also, each condo is equipped entirely with easy-opening leper-safe doors and drawers.

CHUCK: *(To* SHEILA*)* Sounds perfect, honey.

SHEILA: Sure does.

BRYAN: Of course, you're probably also wondering about our medical facilities.

SHEILA: Medical facilities?

BRYAN: Yes.

CHUCK: You mean you've got like a hospital here too?

BRYAN: Well, not a hospital exactly. But we do have a registered nurse and an emergency medical response team on call twenty-four hours a day.

CHUCK: Gosh, I've never heard of anything like that. *(To* SHEILA*)* Isn't that something, hon?

*(*SHEILA *nods.)*

BRYAN: Yes, well of course since we rent exclusively to lepers, we find it necessary to provide for the special needs of our residents.

CHUCK: Oh, uh, of course. *(To* SHEILA*)* Isn't that wonderful, Sheila?

SHEILA: So thoughtful.

*(*CHUCK *wipes tears from his eyes.)*

CHUCK: Thank God we found this place.

*(*SHEILA *comforts him.)*

SHEILA: It's okay, honey. It's gonna be okay. *(To* BRYAN*)* You mentioned the application?

BRYAN: Yes. Of course. First, I'll just need to see your medical records.

SHEILA: Our what?

BRYAN: Medical...records. You know, from the doctor.

SHEILA: Oh.

CHUCK: What do you need those for?

BRYAN: Well, it is an important part of the application process.

SHEILA: Aren't our records supposed to be private?

BRYAN: Yes, that's right. I can't force you to share that information but then I also can't approve your application without proof of your condition.

CHUCK: So all you need is proof we have leprosy?

BRYAN: Exactly.

CHUCK: Well, that's no problem. *(Beat)* Look at us.

BRYAN: *(Nervous laugh)* Yes, well I'm afraid I need official documentation.

SHEILA: We don't have any.

BRYAN: You don't have any?

SHEILA: We haven't been to a doctor.

BRYAN: You haven't?

SHEILA: We were too embarrassed.

CHUCK: *(Overlapping)* It wasn't covered by our H M O.

SHEILA: Right.

BRYAN: Well, if you haven't been to a doctor, how do you know you even have leprosy?

SHEILA: Look at us.

BRYAN: Yes, I know, obviously I can see that you have some kind of...condition, but without professional medical diagnosis, how do you know it's not a rash or something else?

CHUCK: *(Indignant)* Look, buddy. Uh... *(Faltering)* My, uh...my big toe fell off last week. You call that a rash?

(SHEILA looks at CHUCK, surprised.)

BRYAN: Your toe fell off and you didn't go to a doctor?

SHEILA: We've been trying homeopathic remedies.

BRYAN: *(Suspiciously)* Such as?

(CHUCK and SHEILA look at one another quickly.)

CHUCK: Tea.

SHEILA: Yes, tea.

BRYAN: Tea.

CHUCK: Lots of tea.

BRYAN: Well listen, I'm afraid there's nothing—

SHEILA: Why are you doing this to us?

BRYAN: I beg your pardon?

CHUCK: Honey, calm down.

SHEILA: No, I won't calm down, Chuck. *(To BRYAN)* You think this is easy for us? Six months ago my

husband and I were both very successful professionals.
We were young, healthy, financially secure. We had
the perfect life. Then the next thing we knew we'd lost
everything we worked for and dreamed about to this
horrible, medieval disease. Now you sit there giving us
this bureaucratic bull...shit. My husband's finger—

CHUCK: Toe—

SHEILA: —toe fell off, dammit. *(Getting angrier)* And
if we have to have some damn piece of paper from a
doctor to prove to you that we've suffered enough to
deserve to live here, then you can take your little leper
condo and you can just...shove it!

(SHEILA breaks down. CHUCK comforts her.)

CHUCK: It's okay, honey. It's okay. *(To BRYAN, angrily)* I
hope you're proud of yourself.

BRYAN: *(Contrite)* Mister and Mrs Phillips, I'm terribly
sorry. You know, sometimes in this line of work it's
easy to forget that people are more important than
procedures. I'll tell you what I can do. I'm going to
recommend you for an exemption on the medical
documentation clause. I'll speak to the manager about
it personally.

CHUCK: Thank you.

SHEILA: I'm sorry I lost my temper.

BRYAN: No, Mrs Phillips. I'm sorry. Please forgive me.

CHUCK: You were just trying to do your job.

SHEILA: We understand.

(BRYAN hands them a form.)

BRYAN: All I need you to do is sign on the dotted line
at the bottom there and we can have your application
processed within forty-eight hours.

CHUCK: Great.

SHEILA: God bless you, Bryan.

(BRYAN *smiles warmly at both of them. He hands* CHUCK *a pen. Just as* CHUCK *starts to sign the paper,* BRYAN *suddenly reaches across the desk. He grabs* CHUCK *by the arm and forcefully rips away a layer of scar tissue.* CHUCK *is so stunned that at first he doesn't react. Then, after a beat,* SHEILA *cues him by tapping his leg with the back of her hand.* CHUCK *screams in fake pain.)*

CHUCK: Ow!

BRYAN: Aha! *(He holds the handful of fake scar tissue under his nose and sniffs it.)* Spirit gum!

(CHUCK *tries to grab the scar tissue away from* BRYAN.)

CHUCK: Give me that!

BRYAN: Did you really think you could get away with this? You think I couldn't tell this was latex? I was a drama major in college, for crying out loud.

SHEILA: Please! We've been through so much—

BRYAN: Quiet lady! You're no more a leper than I am. Get out of here. Get out of my office!

CHUCK: You're going to hear from my lawyer. We have the same rights to that condo as anyone else. Discrimination is illegal.

BRYAN: Yeah, well so's impersonating a leper, buddy! Go on, get outta here!

(CHUCK *and* SHEILA *get up and leave.)*

BRYAN: *(Yelling after them)* You should be ashamed of yourselves!

(BRYAN *sits down at his desk. After a moment, the phone rings.)*

BRYAN: Hello, Leper Valley Condo Association. *(Listens)* Yes, that's right, we are the premiere private leper community in the Northeast. *(Listens)* What's

that? Weight room? *(Angrily)* Nice try, Yuppie
scumbag!

(BRYAN *slams the phone down. Blackout)*

END OF PLAY

WHITE TRASH BINGO

WHITE TRASH BINGO was first produced by the Subterranean Theater Company, Los Angeles in 1996:

LORETTA .... Tania Gutsche
KRYSTAL .... Sarah Anderson
EARL JR .... Tom Geha
EARL.. Tom Sonnek

Director .... Chrissy Sonnek

Scene One

(Lights up on a mobile home somewhere in America. LORETTA *sits on the couch. She wears a tattered bathrobe. On the coffee table in front of her are stacks of several hundred Lotto game cards.)*

(With a quarter, LORETTA *furiously rubs off the spaces on each card, examines it, then throws it on the floor. She remains single-mindedly obsessed with this activity throughout the play.)*

*(*KRYSTAL *enters. She is sixteen, barefoot, and pregnant.)*

KRYSTAL: Mom, Earl Junior's doin' nasty stuff with the cat again.

LORETTA: Tell him not to bring it in the house.

KRYSTAL: I told him that cat was gonna bite his thing off if he don't quit it.

(Off-stage, we hear EARL JR *scream.* EARL JR *runs on-stage, one hand holding his overalls up, the other clutching his groin. He runs across the stage and exits on the other side.)*

KRYSTAL: I told ya!

*(*EARL *enters. He is an overweight man in his mid-to-late thirties. He wears only a pair of what were once white underwear. He eats from a bag of pork rinds. On his bare chest are several surgery scars.)*

EARL: What's wrong with him?

KRYSTAL: Cat bit his thing off, I reckon.

EARL: I knew we shoulda got a dog.

(EARL *sits in a chair and eats pork rinds.*)

KRYSTAL: Daddy, you know you ain't supposed to be eatin' that.

EARL: Who says?

KRYSTAL: Doctor told you if you had another heart attack you was gonna die.

EARL: *(Pointing to scars)* First seven didn't kill me.

(EARL JR *walks through with a gun and exits.*)

KRYSTAL: Eight, Daddy.

EARL: *(With mouth full)* Who's countin'?

KRYSTAL: Tell him, Mom.

LORETTA: Eat up, Earl.

(*Off-stage, we hear a gunshot.* EARL JR *enters with the dead cat in a Wal-Mart bag.*)

EARL JR: Hey Mom, how 'bout I cook dinner tonight?

LORETTA: That's sweet, honey. Thanks.

EARL JR: You bet.

(EARL JR *exits.*)

LORETTA: He's a good boy.

(KRYSTAL *starts to cry.*)

EARL: What's the matter with you?

KRYSTAL: I wish I wasn't havin' a baby.

LORETTA: Your brother said he was sorry, Krystal.

(EARL *is suddenly seized by a massive chest pain. He clutches his chest.* KRYSTAL *rushes to him.*)

KRYSTAL: Daddy!

(LORETTA *rubs off another card. She becomes excited.*)

LORETTA: Woo hoo!

KRYSTAL: Daddy?

(EARL coughs out a half-chewed wad of pork rind and breathes freely.)

EARL: Went down the wrong pipe.

(LORETTA takes another look at the card. Her spirits fall. She throws the card on the floor.)

LORETTA: Shit.

(EARL eats more pork rinds. Blackout)

Scene Two

(Lights up. EARL JR is sitting between EARL and LORETTA. EARL now drinks a beer in addition to eating pork rinds.)

EARL JR: Hey Dad, I think I got somethin' wrong with me. Some kind of rash or somethin'.

(EARL looks at him, keeps munching.)

EARL JR: I think maybe I got it from that cat. When it bit me.

EARL: Let's see.

(EARL JR pulls his shoe off. His foot is swollen and has turned a grotesque green color with oozing sores.)

EARL JR: It's all down my whole leg.

EARL: Hey Loretta.

LORETTA: What?

EARL: Look at this boy's leg.

LORETTA: *(Glances)* You better put somethin' on that.

EARL JR: Okay.

(EARL JR stands and hobbles off-stage. KRYSTAL enters. She carries a baby wrapped in a blanket.)

KRYSTAL: I had my baby.

LORETTA: *(Without looking up)* 'Bout time.

(KRYSTAL *looks at the baby.*)

KRYSTAL: It's sorta...funny lookin'.

EARL: Let's see.

(KRYSTAL *crosses to* EARL *and shows him the baby.*)

KRYSTAL: It's kinda green.

EARL: Hey Loretta.

LORETTA: What?

EARL: Look at this thing.

LORETTA: *(Glances)* It's got Earl Junior's coloring.

KRYSTAL: I gotta go to school. We got a test. Teacher says if I don't pass I gotta do eighth grade again.

(KRYSTAL *puts the baby on the floor and starts to exit.*)

EARL: Hey!

(KRYSTAL *turns.*)

EARL: Bring me a pack of smokes, would ya?

KRYSTAL: You ain't supposed to smoke, Daddy.

EARL: Come on, kiddo. One pack ain't gonna kill me.

KRYSTAL: Mom...

LORETTA: Smoke up, Earl.

EARL: Pack of Lucky's, kiddo. Thanks a million.

(KRYSTAL *exits.*)

LORETTA: *(Mumbles to herself)* A million dollars. Jackpot. Bingo.

EARL: Did ya win?

LORETTA: Not yet.

(EARL *guzzles beer.*)

(*Blackout*)

Scene Three

(LORETTA *rubs off Lotto cards.* EARL *drinks beer, eats pork rinds, and smokes a cigarette.* KRYSTAL *enters and picks up the baby.*)

KRYSTAL: There's somethin' ain't right about this thing. It don't make no noise. Don't cry or nothin'. Don't even move. Just lays around all green and stupid actin'. I knew it'd take after its daddy. It ain't no account at all. *(She exits with the baby.)*

EARL: Hey Loretta.

LORETTA: What?

EARL: What are you gonna do if you win?

LORETTA: Leave.

EARL: Yeah?

LORETTA: Yeah.

(EARL JR *enters. His left leg has fallen off.*)

EARL JR: I think my rash is getting' worse. I was takin' a bath and my leg fell off. It's in there floatin' in the tub. I don't feel good.

LORETTA: You better go lay down.

EARL JR: Okay.

(EARL *finishes his beer and crushes the can. He throws it on the floor.*)

EARL: Bring me another beer first, would ya?

(Off-stage we hear a gunshot.)

EARL JR: Sure Dad.

(EARL JR *hops off-stage on one leg.* KRYSTAL *enters carrying a Wal-Mart bag.*)

KRYSTAL: Who wants supper?

LORETTA: No thanks.

KRYSTAL: Daddy?

(EARL *holds up his bag of pork rinds.*)

EARL: All set, kiddo. Thanks.

(KRYSTAL *exits.* EARL JR *hops on with a beer. He gives it to* EARL.)

EARL JR: Here ya go, Pop.

EARL: Thanks buddy.

EARL JR: You bet.

EARL: Take it easy on that leg, Sport.

EARL JR: Okay.

(EARL JR *hops off-stage.* EARL *opens the beer.*)

EARL: Why would you wanna leave?

(*Blackout*)

Scene Four

(LORETTA *is still rubbing off cards.* EARL *sits motionless in his chair, looking sick.* KRYSTAL *sits in the floor eating from a bowl.* EARL JR *enters. His left arm is in a sling. He scratches maniacally.*)

EARL JR: It's on my arm now.

LORETTA: Don't scratch, honey. You'll make it worse.

EARL JR: (*Looking at* EARL) What's wrong with Dad? He looks green.

EARL: (*With great difficulty*) Ate...too...much.

KRYSTAL: (*To* EARL JR) Hungry?

(EARL JR *doesn't answer. He scratches. Suddenly,* EARL *grabs his chest. All look at him.* EARL *has a heart attack and dies.*)

(*Beat*)

(They all continue.)

KRYSTAL: I'm starvin'. (She plunges her face down into the bowl and eats.

(EARL JR scratches his arm until it falls off in the floor. He stares at it.)

EARL JR: Uh-oh.

(LORETTA rubs off a card. She looks at it. Stops. Looks again. She slowly rises off the couch. She begins to tremble. She throws her arms into the air, triumphantly.)

LORETTA: YES!

(Blackout)

END OF PLAY

THE ROAD IS AN ASPHALT HOSTESS

THE ROAD IS AN ASPHALT HOSTESS was first produced by the Subterranean Theater Company, Los Angeles in 1996:

Performer .... Tom Geha

Director .... Tom Sonnek

Percussion .... Eric Bricker

On a night as dark as nothing,
it rains like that's all it's ever done.
But you still smell the diesel,
and I watch it dance with the water
across the parking lot of a truck stop
someone never got around to naming.
Cave fish in Cadillacs
and trucks
and vehicles of all dimensions -
drawn instinctively to the Neon Womb;
receive Communion from the Waitress,
who renames them after their consumptive
predilections:
"I christen thee Decaf with Danish."
"Thou shalt be called Western Hold the Onions."
Beneath a fluorescent halo,
an off-duty cop coughs
like a cat in a fan belt.
I halt my prayer
to the Caffeine God
to watch his mouth discharge his lungs
onto a plate of steak and eggs;
floating in black Marlboro phlegm.
You call from a phone booth.
(An admirable impression of your own voice.)
You want to talk about the highways.
"The road", you say, "is an asphalt hostess".
A Rest-Stop Epiphany
on a Pilgrimage of Motion.

I respond from a convenience store in Alabama
with a postcard depicting the scenic beauty
and natural wonder
of convenience stores in Alabama -
A dynamic collage:
State of the art gasoline pumps.
A plethora of automotive products.
Immaculate Restroom Facilities.
And a dazzling array of tasty snack treats,
any of which could be safely consumed
by my descendants
for generations to come,
entirely without fear.
I drive away,
with the wailing souls of dinosaurs
drowning in my tank.
You stop in some out-of-the-way flea market to buy
a velvet self-portrait of the King from the nicotine-
stained artist who tells you the one about the once-
proud Western Princess and the Sparkling Men,
who came from Outer Space, and seduced her with
promises and tricks of light, leaving their seed to grow
inside her, spawning mutants in the spring.
And I have a good laugh about that one.
Later.
In my Motorist Hotel room.
With my maps.
And my doubts.
And my gods.
And my travel toothbrush.
And then the Dream.
The one we hate.
We're in the car.
Dad's there behind the wheel.
Big.
Shiny.

Black.
`57 Buick.
American car.
But suddenly we blink.
And Dad's gone.
And we're driving.
And we didn't have power steering then.
We didn't have a lot of things.
Like microwaves.
Or the Beatles.
And the last thing we see is us
falling into the Grand Canyon,
while Mom snaps a Polaroid.
And we wake up screaming.
Different beds.
Different cities.
Different lives.
Separated
by our vast American distance.

BUFFALO ROAM

BUFFALO ROAM was first produced by the
Subterranean Theater Company, Los Angeles in 1996:

STAN .... Jason Farmer
NICK...Matt Caton

Director.. Barrington Smith.

(*Lights up on* STAN *and* NICK. *They stand in front of an imaginary window, looking into the audience.*)

STAN: Now do you believe me?

NICK: Damn.

STAN: I told you. Didn't I? You didn't believe me.

NICK: I mean…damn.

STAN: "Stan, you're full of shit", you told me.

NICK: I don't believe it.

STAN: You see it, don't you?

NICK: Yeah. I see it.

STAN: Well...

NICK: But I don't believe it.

STAN: Believe it, pal. What you see is what you see.

NICK: There must be hundreds of them.

STAN: (*Laughs*) Hundreds? Try thousands. Millions even, maybe.

NICK: They're running right down the middle of the street.

STAN: Now I guess you see who's full of shit and who's not.

NICK: This can't be happening.

STAN: Maybe next time you'll believe me when I tell you there's a gigantic herd of buffaloes running down the street.

NICK: I think it's just "buffalo".

STAN: What? Are you gonna tell me you don't see more than one?

NICK: No, I mean I think even when it's more than one you still just say "buffalo."

STAN: *(Pointing)* That, my friend is more than "buffalo." That is buffa*loes*.

NICK: Maybe we should call somebody. The cops or somebody.

STAN: *(Laughs)* Call the cops. That's rich. Go ahead, Nick. Call the cops, why don't ya?

NICK: I just thought maybe somebody should call somebody.

STAN: What the hell do you think the cops are gonna do about this?

NICK: I don't know.

STAN: Besides, I think even the cops will notice a couple million buffalo running down the street.

NICK: You see? You just said it yourself.

STAN: I said what?

NICK: You said "a couple million *buffalo*".

STAN: So?

NICK: That's what you're supposed to say.

STAN: That's what I said.

NICK: Not before. Before you said buffa*loes*.

STAN: I don't think this is a time to stand and argue grammar.

(NICK *and* STAN *both look out the window.*)

NICK: Where do you think they came from?

STAN: Oh, they probably just took the cross-town bus over from the mall. Where do you think they came from?

NICK: I don't know.

STAN: I didn't think so.

NICK: Do you know?

STAN: Of course I know.

NICK: Where?

STAN: They're obviously from out of town.

NICK: Oh, no shirt, Shitlock. You know what I think?

STAN: Enlighten me.

NICK: I think this is some kind of experience.

STAN: You don't say.

NICK: Some kind of supernatural experience, I mean.

STAN: Yeah, it's the friggin' Twilight Zone. *(Points)* Look, there's Rod Sterling bringing up the rear.

NICK: I'm serious. It's like some kind of sign.

STAN: Of what?

NICK: I don't know. Something. Something important.

STAN: Probably somebody making a movie.

NICK: It's an omen. That's what it is.

STAN: You read too much.

NICK: No, really Stan. I'm getting these, these vibes.

STAN: Vibes?

NICK: Yeah. These buffaloes running down the street in the middle of broad daylight isn't just some kind of coincidence. It's definitely a sign of something.

STAN: Sure. Let's get back to work.

NICK: Maybe it's the end of the world or something. Christ, I bet it means it's the end of the world, Stan.

STAN: That's nuts.

NICK: How do you know?

STAN: Where does it say anything about buffaloes in the Bible?

NICK: So? That doesn't mean anything.

STAN: You know, Nick, maybe you're right. Maybe it is a sign. I think it is. I think it's a sign we've been working too hard. Let's go get a beer. What do you say?

NICK: Look! They're running from West to East.

STAN: Yeah?

NICK: They're coming to take back the city.

STAN: What do buffaloes want with this town?

NICK: Maybe not this one. *(Thinks)* Oh my God!

STAN: What?

NICK: Think about it. What city is east of here?

STAN: Cleveland?

NICK: Farther.

STAN: What?

NICK: Buffalo. Buffalo, New York.

STAN: Oh come on.

NICK: That's it. It's gotta be. It's a pilgrimage.

STAN: Nick, it's just a bunch of buffalo running down the street. Don't get so worked up.

NICK: Look out there. Look! They keep coming. Miles and miles of them.

STAN: Yeah.

NICK: This is not normal! Something is happening here.

STAN: Maybe it's some kind of atmospheric thing.

NICK: Could be.

STAN: Maybe it's gonna rain.

NICK: I think it's gonna do a lot more than that, Stan.

STAN: Sure are a lot of them, aren't there?

NICK: Where the hell are the cops? Why isn't somebody doing something?

STAN: What can you do?

NICK: It's the end of the world. I'm sure of it.

STAN: How do you know that? Maybe it's something good.

NICK: Something good?

STAN: Yeah. Who says it has to be some kind of catastrophic thing? Maybe it's a *positive* sign.

NICK: Yeah. Maybe so.

STAN: Maybe these buffaloes are peaceful.

NICK: Yeah.

STAN: Hell, they could be from another planet for all we know.

NICK: Buffalo from another planet?

STAN: Who's to say?

NICK: Not me.

STAN: Could be they've come here to teach us the secret of ever-lasting peace or some shit like that.

NICK: Yeah, that's the idea. Positive thinking. I like that.

STAN: Maybe it's supposed to remind us to respect the Earth and take care of the environment. Something like that.

NICK: Yeah. Maybe it's meant to remind us of our own individual capacity for freedom and beauty.

STAN: That's good. I like that.

NICK: Yeah. I mean, look at them. They aren't hurting anybody. They're not damaging any public property.

STAN: Yeah.

NICK: It's definitely some kind of good sign.

STAN: Sure.

NICK: It is.

STAN: Probably.

NICK: No, it is.

STAN: Or maybe—

NICK: No, come on now—

STAN: It could be—

NICK: Don't say it.

STAN: Maybe it's just a bunch of buffaloes running down the street.

(Pause)

NICK: You had to say it.

STAN: I'm just trying to be rational.

NICK: Of course.

STAN: Maybe it's a sign of nothing.

NICK: I don't believe that.

STAN: Maybe not.

NICK: *Definitely* not.

STAN: You're probably right.

NICK: It *means* something.

STAN: Yeah.

NICK: Something important.

STAN: It probably is a sign.

NICK: Yes.

STAN: Of something.

NICK: It's a sign.

STAN: Sure.

NICK: An omen.

STAN: Right.

NICK: I'm sure of it.

STAN: It's definitely a significant event of some kind.

NICK: Absolutely.

(NICK *and* STAN *stare out the window. Lights fade to black.*)

END OF PLAY

PABLO PICASSO TEACHES HIGH SCHOOL

PABLO PICASSO TEACHES HIGH SCHOOL is
unproduced.

This play is dedicated to Joanne Troxel.

(Scene: A high school principal's office. FAY, the principal, sits behind the desk. She presses a button on the intercom.)

FAY: *(Into intercom)* Mister Roberts?

VOICE ON INTERCOM: *(O S)* Yes, Principal Fowler?

FAY: *(Into intercom)* Could you send in the next substitute teacher applicant please?

VOICE ON INTERCOM: *(O S)* Yes ma'am.

(PABLO PICASSO enters. FAY stands to greet him, shakes his hand.)

FAY: Hello. I'm Principal Fowler.

PICASSO: Pablo Picasso.

FAY: It's a pleasure to meet you, Mister Picasso.

(PICASSO doesn't let go of her hand. He kisses it. FAY is surprised and slightly taken back by this, but doesn't entirely mind it.)

PICASSO: *(Notices artwork on wall)* Who painted that piece of shit?

FAY: Oh. That's some of my daughter Shiloh's artwork. She's nine.

PICASSO: She paints like a retarded pig.

FAY: Well, that seems like a bit of a harsh judgment to pass on the artwork of a fourth grader.

PICASSO: Forgive me. I meant only "pig".

FAY: Yes. Well, speaking of art, Mister. Picasso, why don't you have a seat?

PICASSO: *(Sits)* Okay.

FAY: So I see on your application that you're interested in doing some substitute teaching for our art classes.

PICASSO: Yes.

FAY: And I was just wondering if you could tell me a little about yourself.

PICASSO: About me?

FAY: Yes. What's your background in art? What makes you interested in that particular subject? What are your qualifications?

PICASSO: You are serious?

FAY: Yes. It's just a standard part of the interview.

PICASSO: Do you know who I am?

FAY: Well, I see on your form here that you've identified yourself as *Pablo Ruiz y Picasso.* Born October 25, 1881 in Málaga, Spain. Hey, can this be right? According to this, you're a hundred and twenty-six years old.

PICASSO: Yes. That is correct.

FAY: Well, pardon me for indulging momentarily in personal comment, but you look fantastic for a man your age.

PICASSO: You should see me in the nude.

FAY: My goodness, sir. I'll have none of that talk in my office please.

PICASSO: What did I say?

FAY: There's no place in a professional work environment for sexually intimidating speech, Mister Picasso.

PICASSO: There is no reason to be intimidated, Principal Fowler. It's true that I am still a tiger in the bedroom, despite my advanced age. But I assure you… I am a gentle predator.

FAY: Well, I appreciate that clarification, Mister—

PICASSO: Please. Call me Pablo.

FAY: But I think I'd still like to hear a little more about your experience and qualifications.

PICASSO: You want to hear about my qualifications?

FAY: Yes, please.

PICASSO: I am the greatest artist of the twentieth century. That is my qualification.

FAY: Uh huh. And so, when you say "greatest artist of the twentieth century", are you referencing a specific award or commendation? Or could you provide me with the name of the organization or professional service group that honored you?

PICASSO: I don't know what are you saying.

FAY: Well, who says you were the greatest artist of the twentieth century?

PICASSO: What do you mean who says? Everybody! That's who. I am one of the most famous, and most important, artists of all time. Anyone who knows anything can tell you this.

FAY: Yes, I understand. It's just that self-confidence is great, but I'm looking for some documentation of your credentials.

PICASSO: Have you tried Googling "Picasso"?

FAY: We'll come back to that, Mister Picasso. First, can you tell me, have you completed your teacher certification? Because I see that box isn't checked on page seven of your application.

PICASSO: You are asking me for what?

FAY: Teacher certification. You can't teach without it.

PICASSO: How can I get this?

FAY: Well, in order to be certified, you have to take a series of classes from an accredited institution of teacher training.

PICASSO: I have to take classes from someone else before I can teach art?

FAY: That's right.

PICASSO: Did I mention that I was Picasso?

FAY: Yes, but—

PICASSO: Why?

FAY: I beg your pardon?

PICASSO: Why I must do this "certification"?

FAY: Well, as principal, I am responsible for making sure that every teacher who walks into one of our classrooms is fully qualified to execute the educational mission of our school.

PICASSO: You must ensure that the teacher knows the subject well and is able to teach it to the children?

FAY: Of course.

PICASSO: Then your problem is solved.

FAY: I don't understand.

PICASSO: You need someone to teach art class, yes?

FAY: We do.

PICASSO: And you need to make sure that this person knows art?

FAY: Well, yes, but—

PICASSO: Who is better qualified to teach a high school art class than Picasso!?! The greatest artist of all time! It's all good. "No worries," as the kids say. I will teach your class.

FAY: Well, I'm afraid that won't be possible without the certification.

PICASSO: Madame, art cannot be certified.

FAY: Pablo, it's not that I don't appreciate your passion—

PICASSO: *(Takes her hand)* Then, please, let us discuss this matter in a more, what would you say, "relaxing" atmosphere.

FAY: *(Takes her hand away, eventually)* You don't understand. I have to hire someone to teach this class who has proper paperwork verifying certification. Then that person has to teach the class so that every student in it can get a passing score on a national standardized art test. If you don't take the certification classes and get the piece of paper, I couldn't hire you to teach a high school art class even if you *were* the greatest artist of the twentieth century.

PICASSO: But I *am* the greatest artist of the twentieth century! That's what I'm trying to tell you! And you, you act as if you've never heard of me! You have no idea what an extraordinary thing this is that the great artist Picasso—who was thought to have died in France in 1973—is, in fact, still alive, and has walked into your stupid ugly office offering to teach your retarded pig children about art!

FAY: Mister Picasso, I have to tell you that, even if you weren't completely unqualified and uncertified as a licensed teacher in this state, I would still have grave reservations about trusting someone with your unstable temperament to teach our precious children.

PICASSO: Your children eat puke and dream manure. You suck their hearts out with your tests.

FAY: An educational system must have standards, Mr. Picasso.

PICASSO: An artist must piss on your standards.

FAY: But an art teacher may not even say "piss",
Picasso.

PICASSO: Then you're teaching them death. Not art.

FAY: I have a job to do. Have a good day.

PICASSO: You're saying the interview is done?

FAY: That's what I'm saying.

PICASSO: Then I must apologize. My behavior was
uncalled for. Please forgive me.

FAY: Well…thanks.

PICASSO: I understand that you are only doing your job.

FAY: I appreciate you saying that.

PICASSO: Your job is very hard.

FAY: Well, it could be worse. It's never boring.

PICASSO: I'm sure it is not. Perhaps what you need,
though, is a chance to…"relax".

FAY: Huh. I can't remember the last time I "relaxed".

(PICASSO *starts to rub* FAY's *shoulders. She starts to object
at first, but then doesn't.*)

PICASSO: Then you should let Picasso teach you. If
there is anything I know better than art, it is "relaxing".

FAY: Well, it's not like I can just leave my job in the
middle of the day. I mean…

(PICASSO *takes her hand and kisses it.*)

PICASSO: But Principal Fowler, who is to say that we
could not "relax" right here…on top of your desk?

FAY: Oh my.

PICASSO: Believe me…when it comes to "relaxing", I
am more than certified.

FAY: Oh…how can I say "no" to Picasso?

(FAY and PICASSO kiss passionately, knock stuff off the desk. She lies down on the desk. He is starting to unbutton his shirt.)

PICASSO: Now, my darling, I will show you great art.

FAY: Just one thing.

PICASSO: Yes?

FAY: Have you been tested?

PICASSO: Tested?

(Blackout)

END OF PLAY

THE BASTARD CHILD OF
EVEL KNIEVEL

THE BASTARD CHILD OF EVEL KNIEVEL was first produced by the Subterranean Theater Company, Los Angeles in 1996:

EMILY .... Sarah Anderson

Director .... Reva Fox

EMILY: The kitchen smells like bacon and eggs and there's a small hole in the door where she threw the skillet. Down the sides of the counter, on the refrigerator, and across the floor, there's crispy black pieces of meat and yellow fluffed-up egg balls trapped in little lakes of bacon grease that's turned white and solid.

Marlene's smoking Marlboro after Marlboro and the ashes are falling onto her ragged yellow bath robe. The front door's standing open with the fan in front of it blowing hot air out and sucking flies in through the busted screen.

I'm sitting on the floor in front of her. People standing around some kind of rocket on T V. Marlene says it ain't the moon, it's Idaho. She traces her finger over the duct tape patch on the ripped vinyl of the couch. She shifts the cigarette to her other hand and plays with my hair.

"You're supposed to call me Mommy."

I tap my fingers against the stack of *Reader's Digest Condensed Books* from the Goodwill under the couch where the leg used to be. I don't say anything.

He's out in the driveway, cursing and pounding with his rusty socket wrenches on the engine of the girl's Camaro. She's standing beside him, in her tank top and cut-off jeans, knocking her class ring against the front fender. I get away from the door like I'm told. Marlene strikes another match.

"Turn up the TV, kiddo."

Then she points: "Look honey, there he is."

I look at the television. A white leather American flag
with feet struts out of a trailer. People are yelling their
heads off for him. He throws some kind of stick into
the crowd.

"He's throwin' them his cane. He always does that."
But even without it he still seems to walk okay as he
heads toward that spaceship. Marlene says he's not an
astronaut:

"He's a daredevil, baby. He's gonna jump across that
canyon."

Outside, the Camaro's engine coughs, then dies again.
"Ain't he handsome, kiddo?"
She's got tears in her eyes. He climbs up the ramp.
Waves again. I wave back. Marlene smiles and I keep
waving. I'm pretending that's my real daddy there. On
T V.

"Wave, Mommy."
She laughs out loud. And I think she's pretending too.
I rest my head against the sharp hairs on her leg and
hold my breath.

The rocket blasts off as car doors slam in our driveway.
Explosions of orange flame shoot out from behind.
Loose gravel cuts into the aluminum walls of our
trailer. Tires squeal at the first turn in the road and the
parachute opens. We watch him fall. Down into the
canyon. Until he's gone.

Marlene drops her hand to her lap. A long ash breaks
off and disappears between her legs. I turn my head
away and close my eyes.

I can smell the smoke.

END OF PLAY

POETS ANONYMOUS

POETS ANONYMOUS was first produced by the
Vigilante Theater Company, Bozeman (Montana) in
2003:

MANNY.. John Hosking
SVETLANA..Suzanne Fortin
JOLLY ROGER.. David Mills-Low
SIOUX CITY SUE.. Rhonda Smith

Director ....Greg Owens

The sonnet *Proverbial Fuel* is by Greg Keeler

(Scene: The restaurant area of a truck stop. One table. Four chairs. MANNY enters, taking off his apron. He speaks to an unseen character off-stage.)

MANNY: Mae, I'm taking my lunch break now to meet with the group. You got it covered? *(Listens, responds)* Thanks Mae. I'll see ya.

(MANNY shuts kitchen door. Business placing chairs, etc. He doesn't notice SVETLANA enter. She is a Ukranian woman, dressed very stylishly; designer jeans, extravagant boots, expensive jewelry.)

SVETLANA: *(Smiling)* Hello Manny.

(MANNY looks up. He doesn't seem as happy to see SVETLANA.)

MANNY: Hi.

SVETLANA: Manny, are you mad at me?

MANNY: Why would I be mad?

SVETLANA: You know why. Because of last week.

MANNY: It's been a week since then. I don't remember it.

SVETLANA: Manny, please don't be mad at me.

MANNY: Fine. I won't be mad.

(Pause)

SVETLANA: *(Sitting)* Manny, make me a hamburger.

MANNY: What?

SVETLANA: Please.

MANNY: I'm on break.

SVETLANA: Manny, please, get me a hamburger. I'm hungry. I don't have anything to eat at home.

MANNY: I thought your husband was rich. Why don't you tell him to buy you some food?

SVETLANA: He doesn't let me eat. He watches me like crow.

MANNY: You mean hawk?

SVETLANA: That too. Ever since my mother came last year to visit from Ukraine, my husband he's paranoid I'm going to become big like Momma. Even if I eat just one box of Ding Dongs. Or one hamburger.

MANNY: Sounds like a heckuva guy.

SVETLANA: Manny, don't start that again.

MANNY: I'm not starting anything, Svetlana.

SVETLANA: Manny, I know you are in love with me, but there's nothing I can do about it.

MANNY: Don't flatter yourself.

SVETLANA: I cannot betray my marriage to Bud.

MANNY: *(Scoffs)* "Marriage."

SVETLANA: We are married. And Bud is the one who brought me to this country.

MANNY: You mean mail ordered you.

SVETLANA: He saved my life.

MANNY: Good for him. Too bad he won't feed you.

SVETLANA: I am tired of this argument. When does the meeting start? Where's Roger and Alice.

MANNY: Alice isn't coming. She called off work again today.

SVETLANA: How come?

MANNY: Sister broke her foot.

SVETLANA: Her sister broke her foot and Alice can't come?

MANNY: That's what she said.

SVETLANA: That woman is a horticultural liar.

MANNY: *(Laughs)* Pathological.

SVETLANA: What?

MANNY: You mean pathological liar.

SVETLANA: Yes.

MANNY: You said—

SVETLANA: What did I say?

MANNY: You said "horticultural."

SVETLANA: What is "horticultural"?

MANNY: Like with plants. Green things that grow.

SVETLANA: Oh. *(Thinks about it, gets tickled)* That's funny.

(MANNY rolls his eyes at SVETLANA.)

SVETLANA: Manny, you like me don't you?

MANNY: No.

SVETLANA: You're a pig.

MANNY: Oink.

(SVETLANA smiles. MANNY smiles. ROGER enters. A truck driver.)

ROGER: Hey guys!

SVETLANA: *(Friendly)* Hi Roger!

ROGER: *(Speaks to an unseen character)* Come on over. It's all right. No need to be scared.

SVETLANA: Roger, who are you talking to?

ROGER: Hope you guys don't mind. I brought a friend.

(SIOUX CITY SUE *enters. She is a homeless vagabond, eccentrically and shabbily dressed. A distant look in her eyes as if she might be a little crazy. Anxious and shy. She carries a tambourine, which she will use later when she becomes more animated.* MANNY *and* SVETLANA *react to seeing* SUE.)

ROGER: Sue, these are my friends. This is Svetlana. And that's Manny. Guys, this is Sue.

SUE: Sioux City Sue.

ROGER: Sioux City Sue, that's right.

SUE: Sioux City Sue is my name.

(SUE *looks at* MANNY *and* SVETLANA *and nods.* MANNY *doesn't know what to say.*)

SVETLANA: Hello Sioux City Sue. *(Offers her hand)* I am Svetlana.

(SUE *smiles suddenly at* SVETLANA *and enthusiastically shakes her hand.*)

SUE: Atlanta.

SVETLANA: Svetlana.

SUE: It's nice to meet you, Georgia.

(SVETLANA *finally breaks her hand free.* SUE *smiles at* ROGER, *who gives her an encouraging smile back.* SUE *crosses to* MANNY *and offers her hand.*)

SUE: Sioux City Sue is my name.

MANNY: *(Without shaking her hand)* Yeah. Nice to meet ya. Manny. *(Gets up from table)* Excuse me. *(Crosses toward* ROGER) Can I talk to you?

(MANNY *and* ROGER *step away from the table.* SUE *sits down.* SVETLANA *watches her as* SUE *takes a salt shaker and begins pouring salt onto the table. With her finger, she starts to arrange the salt on the table into some sort of shape.*)

ROGER: *(Aside with* MANNY) What is it?

MANNY: What did I tell you about bringing people outside the group to the meetings?

ROGER: But Manny, she's—

MANNY: I don't care what her story is, Roger. It's always something with you. When are you gonna quit picking up strays?

ROGER: Manny, that's not very nice.

MANNY: Nice? The homeless derelict you brought in here with you last week bit my finger. Was that nice?

ROGER: Willie didn't mean to bite you.

MANNY: *(Shows him bandage)* Does that look like he didn't mean it to you?

ROGER: Look Manny, I already told you I'm sorry about that. But Sue doesn't have anywhere else to go right now. I'm giving her a ride.

MANNY: One of these wackos you pick up is gonna chop your head off someday, Roger.

ROGER: Don't be so dramatic. Sue's harmless.

(MANNY and ROGER both look over at SUE, making the salt drawing on the table. SVETLANA, who has been watching SUE, looks at ROGER and MANNY.)

MANNY: Harmless, huh? She looks like an ever bigger nut job than last week.

ROGER: People need help, Manny.

MANNY: You need help.

(Pause)

SVETLANA: *(To SUE)* What are you doing?

SUE: *(Sing-song, mostly to her self)* "I think that I shall never see a poem as lovely as a tree."

(SVETLANA recognizes what she's drawing in the salt.)

SVETLANA: Oh. Is that a tree?

SUE: No. It's a poem.

SVETLANA: I see.

MANNY: *(To* ROGER*)* You know I don't like outsiders at the meetings. It makes me self-conscious.

ROGER: Sue's nice. You'll like her.

*(*MANNY *looks at* ROGER, *skeptically.)*

ROGER: Come on. She won't bite.

*(*MANNY *gives* ROGER *a dirty look.)*

ROGER: I hope.

*(*ROGER *slaps* MANNY *playfully on the back and crosses to the table.)*

SUE: *(Greeting* ROGER *warmly)* Jolly Roger!

ROGER: Sioux City Sue!

SUE: Hi.

ROGER: Hi. What you got there?

*(*SUE *looks at the salt. She wets her finger with her tongue. She touches the salt with her finger, then puts it on her tongue. She turns to* ROGER, *answering his question in a matter-o-fact one.)*

SUE: Salt.

ROGER: *(Smiles)* Oh.

SUE: *(Smiles)* Oh.

*(*MANNY *has meantime crossed to the table.)*

MANNY: *(Gruffly, to* SUE*)* Clean that up.

*(*SUE *looks at* MANNY. *Her smile changes into an expression that mocks the stern one on his face. With her hand, she wipes the salt off the table onto the floor. It is not an aggressive, nor violent, gesture, but defiant nonetheless. She and* MANNY *stare at one another.)*

SVETLANA: *(Breaking tension)* Why don't we get started? I have things to do.

(ROGER *sits.*)

MANNY: *(Sitting, sarcastically)* Like what?

SVETLANA: *(Sitting)* Like none of your business.

MANNY: Fine.

SVETLANA: Start the meeting.

ROGER: Isn't Alice coming?

SVETLANA: Her sister broke her foot.

ROGER: Her sister broke Alice's foot?

MANNY: No. She broke her own foot.

ROGER: Alice?

SVETLANA: Sister.

ROGER: Oh.

MANNY: Can we get started?

ROGER: Sure.

MANNY: Okay. I hereby call to order this meeting of the Bud's I-90 Truck Stop Casino Poetry Discussion Group.

ROGER: Hear, hear!

SUE: *(Mimicking him, happily)* Hear, hear! *(She does it to* SVETLANA.) Hear, hear!

SVETLANA: *(Responding to her in kind)* Hear, hear!

SUE: *(To* MANNY) Hear, hear!

MANNY: Whatever. Whose got new stuff to read?

SVETLANA: I do.

MANNY: Me too.

ROGER: Me too.

SUE: *(Following* ROGER) Me too.

MANNY: Right. Who wants to go first?

SVETLANA: I will.

MANNY: Shoot.

SVETLANA: *(Taking out piece of paper)* This is a new poem
I wrote this week about my home: *(Reads)*
I've come so far from my home in Ukraine,
A place, I fear, I shall see not again.
My father's work boots on the hard wood floor,
My mother's soft taps on my bedroom door,
My sister's long hair with the scent of rain;
The sights, sounds, and smells of my home in Ukraine.

ROGER: Bravo.

SVETLANA: Thank you.

SUE: Bravo.

SVETLANA: *(To* SUE*)* Thank you. *(She looks at* MANNY.*)*

MANNY: *(To the group)* Comments?

ROGER: I loved it.

SUE: Me too.

ROGER: Beautiful imagery.

SVETLANA: Thank you. *(To* MANNY*)* What did you
think?

MANNY: I thought it was fine.

SVETLANA: Fine?

MANNY: Yeah. I mean a couple of the rhymes sorta
bugged me.

SVETLANA: What is "bugged"?

MANNY: They bothered me.

SVETLANA: You didn't like it.

MANNY: No, it was fine. It's just, you know—

SVETLANA: What?

MANNY: "Again" doesn't really rhyme with "Ukraine", that's all.

ROGER: Oh come on, Manny—

MANNY: I'm just saying—

SVETLANA: But the letters are the same.

MANNY: Yeah, the letters are the same but they don't rhyme.

SVETLANA: Why not?

MANNY: Because that's English.

SVETLANA: English is dumb.

MANNY: Forget it. I'm sorry I said anything.

SVETLANA: Me too.

SUE: *(Chimes in)* Me too.

(MANNY glares at SUE.)

ROGER: You wanna go next, Manny?

MANNY: What, so she can get back at me by saying she doesn't like mine? No thanks.

SVETLANA: I wouldn't do that.

MANNY: You did last week.

SVETLANA: I didn't like your poem last week.

MANNY: I think you made that clear.

ROGER: *(Trying to smooth things)* Guys, guys! Come on. This is supposed to be fun.

SUE: *(Clapping)* Yay!

MANNY: *(Sarcastically)* Yippee.

SVETLANA: Roger, why don't you go next?

ROGER: All right. Here's one I just made up this morning: *(Recites from memory)*
There once was a lonely old trucker,

His dry cracked old lips he did pucker,
When a pretty young Miss,
Came and gave him a kiss...
And they lived happily ever after.

(SVETLANA *laughs, then* ROGER, *then* SUE. MANNY *doesn't laugh.*)

SVETLANA: That's so funny.

ROGER: *(To* MANNY, *laughing)* I know it doesn't rhyme right.

MANNY: Thankfully.

SVETLANA: *(To* MANNY*)* Come on, Manny. It was funny. Don't be such a mud on the stick.

MANNY: Stick in the mud.

SVETLANA: That too. *(To* ROGER*)* Bravo, Roger.

SUE: *(Clapping)* Bravo!

ROGER: *(Bows his head, graciously)* I thank you.

MANNY: Geez, how could I possibly follow that?

SVETLANA: Come on, Manny. Let's hear yours.

ROGER: Yeah, Manny, let's hear it.

SUE: *(To* MANNY*)* Let's hear it.

(MANNY *glances ruefully at* SUE, *as he turns a page in his notebook.*)

MANNY: Okay, this is a poem about romance.

SVETLANA: Oh, that's sweet.

MANNY: It's called *Love Songs Are Stupid*.

(SUE *rolls her eyes,* MANNY *reads.*)

MANNY: Love songs are stupid;
  when you've got no one to sing them to.
Love songs are stupid;
  when she wouldn't even listen anyway.

Love songs are stupid;
  because people who have love don't need songs.
Love songs are stupid;
  because they make me think of you.

(SVETLANA *has grown increasingly uncomfortable during
the poem. There is palpable tension between her and* MANNY
when he finishes. Neither will look at the other.)

ROGER: Manny, that's beautiful.

MANNY: *(Self-conscious)* Thanks.

SUE: Bravo.

(MANNY *shakes his head, smiles slightly at* SUE.)

MANNY: *(To* SVETLANA*)* Did you hate it?

SVETLANA: No.

MANNY: Well?

SVETLANA: I don't like free verse.

MANNY: Of course.

ROGER: I think it's some of your best work, Manny.

MANNY: Really?

ROGER: You bet.

SUE: Me too.

MANNY: *(To* SUE*)* Thank you.

SUE: *(To* ROGER*)* Me too. Me too.

ROGER: *(Not understanding)* What?

(SUE *stands, recites poem:*)

SUE: We make up stories to relieve our desire, but they
only add the proverbial fuel. Thus
where her hair stops behind her ear, the day
starts for him. His hands do what they must
to keep the world at bay. Her eyes take in
the imagery in blacks and greens, colors forbidden

in the tales of her tribe. What the sun and wind
have done to his face, his offhand words have hidden
in her heart. So when do the stories stop and the
  meanings
start? If only on film, have you watched the blackened
martyr wilt in the truth of fire? Leaning
into the weather have you fallen toward a slackened
wind? To weep at a wedding or at the dire
tune of a funeral is to weep at the end of desire.

(The others sit in stunned, awkward silence as SUE *finishes the poem. She looks at them for some kind of response. No one says anything.* SUE *turns away from them and looks at the floor.)*

MANNY: *(Standing)* Yeah, well, this has been fun, but I gotta get back to work.

SVETLANA: *(Also rising)* Yes. I have to go too. See you next week, Roger.

MANNY: *(To* ROGER*)* Alone.

ROGER: *(Quietly)* All right, guys. I'll see ya later.

SVETLANA: *(To* MANNY, *as they cross away)* Goodbye, Manny.

MANNY: Stick around. I'll make you a hamburger.

SVETLANA: Okay.

*(*SVETLANA *and* MANNY *exit together.* ROGER *slowly rises from the table and crosses to* SUE. *His demeanor has changed. He is not unfriendly with her, but more distant.)*

ROGER: Well, come on, Sue. We better get going.

SUE: *(Without looking up)* Sioux City Sue.

ROGER: I'm sorry. Sioux City Sue.

SUE: Jolly Roger.

ROGER: *(Uncomfortable)* Yep. Well, let's go.

*(*SUE *looks up at him.)*

SUE: Did you like it?

ROGER: *(Hesitates)* It was fine.

SUE: *(Nods)* Fine.

(SUE exits. ROGER follows her. lights fade.)

END OF PLAY

AT THE INTERSECTION OF AGE AND RAGE

AT THE INTERSECTION OF AGE AND RAGE was first produced by the Bloomington Playwrights Project in 2008:

AGE .... Nicole Roeder

RAGE .... Abby Dillion

DIRECTOR .... Jim Hetmer

(Scene: A street corner with a pedestrian crosswalk where sits a pole, attached to which is a button which, when pushed, theoretically, activates the "Walk" sign.)

(RAGE and AGE approach the button at the same time. AGE gestures, indicating that s/he in no way intends to contest RAGE for the privilege of pressing the button. RAGE, nonetheless, inexplicably, reacts with hostility toward AGE, physically threatening and/or making gestures of an extremely rude nature. RAGE then obstinately refuses to push the button. AGE, bewildered, then afraid, next perturbed, pushes the button, then AGE gives RAGE a look of disdainful superiority, which RAGE deflates with a scornful motion of his or her lips, causing AGE to thrust his or her hands into his or her pockets…with ambiguous intensity.)

(Silence)

(Then…)

AGE: That could've been you pushing that button.

RAGE: Fuck off with your button.

(Silence)

(Then…RAGE grows impatient. S/he pushes and/or kicks the button aggressively.)

AGE: You saw me push it.

RAGE: So?

AGE: So you know there's no need.

RAGE: *(Angry)* Need of what?

AGE: *(Correcting)* Need FOR.

RAGE: Need FOR what?

AGE: There's no need for the BUTTON to be pushed a second time. Especially not in such an exceedingly violent manner.

RAGE: I'll fucking show ya a violent manner.

AGE: I'm not afraid of you.

RAGE: You're not, are you?

AGE: No.

RAGE: Better be fucking glad you're not.

AGE: Nice mouth.

RAGE: Look what's in it. *(Sticks tongue out.)*

AGE: Your parents must be proud.

RAGE: That wounded me.

(Silence. RAGE challenges AGE with a look as they both realize the light has still not changed.)

AGE: It is designed to bring on the light with only one push of the button. More than one push is...

RAGE: ...is what? Frivolous?

AGE: Superfluous.

RAGE: But sometimes it doesn't work unless you push it more than once.

AGE: Do you know why that is?

RAGE: No. Why?

AGE: Because OF people who push it more than once.

(Brief silence...then...)

RAGE: Nonetheless, here we are.

AGE: Yes.

RAGE: Both in need of traversing this thoroughfare.

AGE: Indeed.

RAGE: You wish to follow the rules and push the button only once.

AGE: Correct.

RAGE: Whereas I, on the other hand, feel a strong compulsion to follow my own instincts which tell me to… *(Pounding button repeatedly, with increasing fury and intensity)* …PUSH THE FUCKING BUTTON AS MANY FUCKING TIMES AS I FUCKING WELL PLEASE UNTIL I SEE THE FUCKING LIGHT COME ON!

(A long, fraught silence ensues, until…)

AGE: It doesn't seem to have worked.

RAGE: No, but it felt magnificent. *(Starts to cross the street.)*

AGE: Some people believe that feelings and instincts should govern everything.

RAGE: When those possessing neither are clearly the most fit to rule, of course.

(RAGE *"flips"* AGE *off, turns to cross the street. After* RAGE's *back is turn,* AGE *lifts hand, sadly, waves goodbye. Blackout)*

END OF PLAY

www.ingramcontent.com/pod-product-compliance
Lightning Source LLC
Chambersburg PA
CBHW070022110426
42741CB00034B/2305